STERLING CHILDREN'S BOOKS
New York

An Imprint of Sterling Publishing Co., Inc.
1166 Avenue of the Americas
New York, NY 10036

ISBN 978-1-4549-2917-8

Distributed in Canada by Sterling Publishing Co., Inc.
c/o Canadian Manda Group, 664 Annette Street
Toronto, Ontario M6S 2C8, Canada
Distributed in the United Kingdom by GMC Distribution Services
Castle Place, 166 High Street, Lewes, East Sussex BN7 1XU, England
Distributed in Australia by NewSouth Books
45 Beach Street, Coogee, NSW 2034, Australia

For information about custom editions, special sales, and premium and corporate purchases,
please contact Sterling Special Sales at 800-805-5489 or specialsales@sterlingpublishing.com.

Manufactured in China

Lot #:
2 4 6 8 10 9 7 5 3 1
06/18
sterlingpublishing.com

Cover and interior design by Ryan Thomann
Cover and interior illustrations by Laura Horton
The artwork in this book was created digitally.

NeveR

50 Unstoppable Kids Who Made a Difference

Too Young!

by AILEEN WEINTRAUB · illustrated by LAURA HORTON

STERLING CHILDREN'S BOOKS
New York

Contents

» INTRODUCTION «

Have you ever felt like you're too young to do something? That may be true in some ways (you're probably too young to drive a car or own a house!), but you're definitely not too young to make a difference. In this book, you'll meet famous musicians, writers, scientists, athletes, and activists who accomplished great things by the time they were eighteen. These amazing kids changed the world by coming up with new inventions, making art and music, competing in sports, and speaking out about important issues. Some of these kids were alive hundreds of years ago; others are still wowing people with their talents today.

Some of the fascinating kids you'll learn about include a seven-year-old surgeon, a girl who fought for her right to go to school, a rock sensation, an eagle huntress, a soccer legend, and an Olympic gold medalist. You'll also read about a young movie star, a deaf and blind girl who overcame many obstacles, and a boy who builds electronics out of scrap metal.

Are you ready to be impressed and inspired?

Turn the page to find out more about
fifty of the most spectacular kids
you'll ever meet!

1954–

"I don't think that racism has a place in
the hearts and minds of our children."

RUBY BRIDGES
ACTIVIST FOR RACIAL EQUALITY

At six years old, Ruby Bridges was the first African American child to attend an all-white school in New Orleans, Louisiana. Until the 1960s, all the schools in the Southern United States were segregated. This meant that black children and white children had to attend separate schools. A court ruling known as *Brown versus the Board of Education of Topeka, Kansas*, changed this so that black children could attend previously white-only schools. But even after this law went into effect, many people tried to prevent black students from attending white schools.

After making tons of excuses, William Frantz Elementary in New Orleans finally allowed Ruby to attend class. As she and her mother walked to school on that first day, people stood on the sidewalk calling them terrible names. It was so scary and unsafe that every day for the rest of the school year, Ruby and her mother had to be escorted to school by four federal marshals. People across New Orleans protested Ruby's attendance at her new school. Her father was fired from his job, and one grocery store refused to sell food to the family. At school, none of the other children would talk to Ruby, and some parents even pulled their children out. But Ruby remained brave. She ate lunch alone and spent recess with her teacher. She didn't miss a single day of school that year.

Ruby continued her education at William Frantz, and eventually other black children began attending. After graduating from high school, she became a lifelong activist for racial equality. In 1999, she created the Ruby Bridges Foundation. This foundation teaches tolerance and makes changes through education. Ruby will forever be known for championing the rights of children everywhere to receive a good education—regardless of their race.

1996–

"Kids are passionate and can make a difference. It's just a matter of finding out what you care about and focusing on that."

YASH GUPTA

Yash Gupta was a fourteen-year-old practicing tae kwon do when all of a sudden, his glasses got smashed. While he waited for his new pair to arrive, everything was blurry. He had a hard time seeing the blackboard in school, and he had trouble keeping up with his work. That's when he realized that without glasses, it was almost impossible for him to learn.

Yash was happy when his glasses were fixed, but he couldn't stop thinking about what it was like to live without glasses. After doing research, he found out that there were over thirteen million kids in the world who didn't have money to buy glasses. How could they learn at school if they couldn't even see? Yash also discovered that millions more people throw away perfectly good pairs of glasses each year when they get new prescriptions. This gave him an idea. He looked around his house and found more than ten pairs of old glasses. That's when Yash came up with a plan to create Sight Learning, a nonprofit organization that collects and distributes eyeglasses to students in need around the world. As Yash learned, students who can see are able to make the most of their education.

With his father's help, Yash contacted local eye doctors and asked if he could leave boxes at their front desks, so people could donate their old glasses. Soon after that, Yash began traveling to poor countries to fit children for glasses. Since 2010, Sight Learning has collected and donated over sixteen million dollars' worth of eyeglasses. They have given these glasses to students in countries throughout the world, including Haiti, Mexico, Honduras, and India. Yash knows that helping children see is the best way to make sure they have a bright future!

1929–1945

"How wonderful it is that no one has to wait, but can start right now to gradually change the world!"

ANNE FRANK

WRITER

Born in Germany in the 1930s, Anne Frank was an ordinary girl with a loving family. Her life changed forever after Adolf Hitler became the new leader of Germany. Anne's family was Jewish, and Hitler blamed Jewish people for the country's problems. He sent them to concentration camps, where they were forced to work endlessly.

Anne was ten and living in Amsterdam when Hitler invaded Poland, marking the beginning of World War II. On Anne's thirteenth birthday, her family gave her a diary. That same year, her sister Margot was told she would have to go to a concentration camp. That's when Anne's family decided to go into hiding.

The family of four moved into a small space attached to Anne's father's workplace. The space, hidden behind a bookshelf, became known as the Secret Annex. A week later, four more people joined them. It was a cramped space, and there wasn't a lot of privacy. People spoke in whispers so no one would hear them, and they never left the Annex. The only time they saw anyone else was when the few people who were helping them brought food and news of the outside world. These details of the Annex were captured in Anne's diary. She also wrote about the other people she lived with and about her fears. After two years, German troops discovered the hideout and sent everyone to concentration camps. Just days before the war ended, Anne and Margot both got sick and died in one of the camps. Anne was just fifteen years old.

Anne's father, Otto, was the only member of her family who survived the war. When he went back to Amsterdam, a friend surprised him with Anne's diary, which had been miraculously recovered. Otto decided to publish it as *Anne Frank: The Diary of a Young Girl*. It has been published all over the world in many different languages.

Anne had a short life, but her words live on. Her story continues to help educate people about the mistreatment of Jewish people during the war, which is known today as the Holocaust. The Secret Annex is now a museum that you can visit if you wish to learn more about Anne's life.

1950–

"Just love. That's the most important thing. . . .
That's what's gonna see us through."

STEVIE WONDER

MUSICIAN

Stevland Hardaway Judkins lost his eyesight shortly after he was born in 1950, but that didn't slow him down—especially when it came to music. He found his love of music when he was given a harmonica to play at the age of four. By the age of nine, he was playing the drums and the piano, and by the time he turned ten, everyone in his neighborhood loved listening to him sing.

After his family moved from Saginaw, Michigan, to Detroit, a talent scout introduced Stevland to a big producer at Motown Records. The people at Motown changed Stevland's name to Stevie Wonder and gave him his very first recording contract. Stevie was only eleven years old. His career took off, and he began recording one smash hit after another. His very first hit was called "Fingertips." Then came other rhythm and jazz songs like "Uptight (Everything's Alright)" and "Signed, Sealed, Delivered I'm Yours." At the age of twelve, Stevie released his first album, *The Jazz Soul of Little Stevie Wonder*. That same year, he released another album. His third album, *Recorded Live: The 12 Year Old Genius*, reached number one on the charts! This made him the youngest musician in the history of the United States to have a number-one album.

Throughout his career, Stevie was known as a goofball who loved to play jokes on people. One of his biggest goals was to have fun—all while taking his music very seriously. Stevie did things other musicians had never done before. He was one of the only musicians, for example, to play *all* the instruments on his album. He also used synthesizers to give his music a unique electric sound. This creativity paid off. In 1973, at the age of twenty-three, Stevie became the first black musician to win a Grammy Award for Album of the Year. In 1989, he was inducted into the Rock & Roll Hall of Fame. He has won twenty-five Grammy Awards for his music and was honored with a Grammy Lifetime Achievement Award in 1996. Stevie Wonder's successful career has lasted decades, making him one of the most legendary musical artists in the country!

2001–

AISHOLPAN NURGAIV
EAGLE HUNTRESS

Some children ask their parents if they can have a cat or a dog, but Aisholpan, a ten-year-old girl living in the mountains of Mongolia, asked her parents for an eagle. Aisholpan was born into a family of nomadic herders called Kazakh. They live in tents and herd goats and cattle. These herders are well known for their ancient tradition of raising eagles to hunt foxes and other wild game for food and fur.

It was unusual for a woman to train eagles, and many of the men in Aisholpan's community were against the idea. But her father had faith in her; he knew his daughter could do anything that a boy could do, and they soon began the five-year training process.

Aisholpan caught her eagle chick in the wild and named it Aq Qanttari, which means *white wings*. She cared for the chick until it was ready to begin hunting. As an adult eagle, Aq Qanttari weighs fifteen pounds, and his wing span is eight and a half feet across. That's longer than the height of even the tallest basketball player! Aq Qanttari lives with Aisholpan in the family's home, and the two share a close bond.

In 2014, when Aisholpan was thirteen, she became the first Mongolian female in history to enter the Golden Eagle Festival competition. She was the only child competing against forty men. She beat all of them and took the winning title! Aisholpan's story was so unique that filmmakers decided to make a documentary about her called *The Eagle Huntress*. They traveled to her home and spent months with her and Aq Qanttari. The filmmakers couldn't believe how easily Aisholpan rode on horseback or trekked through huge snow drifts in freezing cold weather with a heavy bird attached to her arm!

Aisholpan is one of only two hundred fifty eagle hunters left in the world. She knows that she won't be doing it forever and has said that she wants to become a doctor when she grows up. If she remains determined, she'll achieve whatever she sets her mind to!

1809–1852

LOUIS BRAILLE

INVENTOR

Three-year-old Louis Braille was playing in his father's leather workshop when he accidentally stabbed himself in the eye with a sharp tool. The infection that followed caused him to go blind in both eyes.

In the nineteenth century, there weren't many resources for blind children. Louis couldn't attend ordinary school because it was too difficult for him to learn without eyesight, but at the age of ten, he was given a scholarship to a school for the blind in Paris. The school was one of the first of its kind in the world. There, Louis learned a complicated system of reading that involved making letters out of copper wire. The letters were hard to tell apart, and the long and difficult process of creating each letter made it so there were very few books for blind people to read.

One day, a soldier came to visit Louis's school and told the students how soldiers communicated using a code made up of twelve raised dots, each representing a different part of speech. The system proved too difficult for the army, but it gave twelve-year-old Louis an idea.

Louis simplified the system by using only six dots. He worked on it for years and named the system *braille*, after himself. At nineteen, he published his first book in braille. Unfortunately, most people didn't pay much attention to it, because they had no idea what it was. Even blind schools refused to teach it! But soon, blind people began learning braille on their own. It took years, but braille eventually caught on in France and began changing the way blind people communicated. The best part was that blind people could now use the dots to write their own books!

As a grown-up, Louis became a teacher at the very school where he had been a student. He lived a short life, dying at the age of forty-three. It wasn't until years later that people across the globe began using braille. Louis did not live to see this success, but there is no doubt that he changed the lives of blind people everywhere with his brilliant idea.

1788–1812

SACAGAWEA

EXPLORER

At age 16, Sacagawea played a big part in the Corps of Discovery, an expedition led by Meriweather Lewis and William Clark to map out new land and search for a passage that connected the Atlantic and Pacific oceans. Sacagawea's husband, Toussaint Charbonneau, was the hired interpreter on the expedition, but it was Sacagawea who knew many tribal languages. She was often the spokesperson for the group, explaining the purpose of the expedition and making trades. She was also an expert food gatherer with knowledge of native plants and hidden trails.

Sacagawea brought her and Charbonneau's son, a baby nicknamed Pomp, on their trip. One day, as the group sailed up the Missouri River, their boat nearly overturned during a storm. Water filled the boat, and all the journals and supplies were in danger of being lost. Sacagawea jumped into action, reaching out into the waves to save whatever she could, all while protecting her baby. If it hadn't been for Sacagawea's quick thinking, all the work that they'd done on the expedition would have floated away.

Lewis and Clark never found the passage—because it doesn't exist! They did, however, complete their mission of mapping out the territory. By the time the expedition was over, the group had survived floods, food shortages, and illness. They would never have gotten through these hardships without Sacagawea's help.

Sacagawea later gave birth to a daughter and passed away shortly after, at the age of twenty-five. We remember her for playing a crucial role in this now-famous expedition.

1995–

"Our work has focused on transforming entire communities in sustainable ways, and our work has the ability to have a positive impact on both the current and future generations."

DYLAN MAHALINGAM

PHILANTHROPIST IN THE DIGITAL AGE

Dylan Mahalingam has always loved technology. That's why, at the age of nine, he helped create Lil' MDGs, a company that uses the power of the Internet to make positive change throughout the world. MDGs is short for Millennium Development Goals. These are goals that the United Nations (an organization made up of leaders from 193 countries) set to improve the lives of the poor. Dylan came up with the idea for Lil' MDGs because he wanted to educate, empower, and inspire children to work together to help others.

Through social media sites like Facebook and Twitter, Lil' MDGs has organized over three million children around the world to work on important issues. Lil' MDGs raises money for natural disaster relief, for the environment, and against animal cruelty. It also helps build libraries, playgrounds, and gardens for those in need.

One of Dylan's favorite projects was raising money for Loita Hills Academy, a school in Kenya. His efforts helped the school raise enough money to build three classrooms, an office space, and bathrooms. They also built a medical clinic that the entire community can use. Dylan often traveled to meet the communities he was helping, and one of the most exciting parts of his visits was meeting other kids who shared his passion for improving people's lives. In 2012, when Dylan was seventeen, the organization had over twenty thousand volunteers in thirty-nine countries. Together, these volunteers helped over a million people!

When Dylan wasn't working with his organization, he spent his time playing guitar and drums, and writing songs in his New Hampshire home. He also played tennis and swam, and he even earned a black belt in karate. His hard work helped him win a full scholarship to college, where he studied computer engineering. Today, Dylan continues to work with poor communities in Kenya.

1756–1791

"I pay no attention whatever to anybody's praise or blame.
I simply follow my own feelings."

WOLFGANG AMADEUS MOZART

MUSICIAN

When Wolfgang Amadeus Mozart was four years old, he handed his father Leopold a piece of paper with blots of ink on it. Leopold thought it was just the scribbles of a child, but when he looked closer, he saw that the blots were musical notes! Not only that, but the notes also made sense and created beautiful music. This was Wolfgang's very first concerto.

Wolfgang was born in Austria in 1756. His father was a violinist and a musical composer, and once he realized how talented Mozart was, the two began writing music together. Wolfgang played the piano while his father wrote down the notes. When Wolfgang was six, Leopold took him to perform for the royal courts of Europe. Wolfgang was talented, and everyone wanted to hear his music.

At seven years old, Wolfgang wrote his first symphony, and by the age of twelve he had written an entire opera. He also had another special talent: He could hear a piece of music just once and then write down every single note. His father eventually decided to dedicate all his time to his son's growing career. The two traveled together for years at a time, mostly performing in front of kings and queens.

By the time Wolfgang was seventeen, he had a job playing music for the royal court in Salzburg, Austria. This was a great honor, but after a while, Mozart wanted a new experience. He moved to Vienna, where he became even more famous, but even so, he wasn't making much money. Back then, musicians were considered servants and were not paid well.

As Wolfgang grew older, people weren't as interested in seeing him perform, but he continued writing music anyway. Some of his most famous works, like *The Magic Flute*, were created toward the end of his life. He died at age thirty-five, in the middle of writing *Requiem*. He never finished it, and many people have tried to write their own endings. Throughout his life, Mozart wrote over six hundred pieces of music, and he is still considered one of the greatest composers to have ever lived.

1928-2014

SHIRLEY TEMPLE

ENTERTAINER

Shirley Temple's mother signed her up for dance lessons when she was just three years old. One day, Hollywood movie producers came to her dance studio looking for actors to perform in a series of short movies. When the producers saw Shirley dance, they knew that she'd be a perfect fit. They offered her ten dollars a day. Shirley's parents agreed, and thus was the start of an amazing career.

When Shirley was six, she had a lead role in a movie called *Stand Up and Cheer!* People loved her performance so much that producers made a movie called *Bright Eyes* just so she could star in it. A year later, in 1935, Shirley won a Special Academy Award for her contribution to the film! Audiences loved her witty humor and tap-dancing skills.

Shirley rose to stardom during the Great Depression. This was a time in American history when many people were out of work and very poor. Watching Shirley sing or do one of her tap routines made people forget about their problems for a while. President Franklin D. Roosevelt even nicknamed Shirley "Little Miss Miracle." Her movies made millions of dollars and included hit songs such as "Animal Crackers in My Soup." Some people say that she saved the film company Twentieth Century Fox from going out of business. By the time Shirley was ten years old, she was one of the highest-paid people in the country and had starred in over forty movies. She was so famous, the Brown Derby Restaurant in Hollywood, California, named a drink after her. Now you can order a Shirley Temple almost anywhere!

Unfortunately, Shirley's success in Hollywood didn't last as she grew up. After starring in a movie that flopped, Twentieth Century Fox canceled her contract, and none of her movies after that did very well. As an adult, Shirley chose a career in public service. She even ran for Congress and served as a US ambassador! She spoke about protecting the environment and helping refugees (people escaping their home countries because of war). In 2005, Shirley won a Lifetime Achievement Award for all her hard work. She died at the age of eighty-five in her California home.

1880–1968

"If we work long enough and earnestly enough, we can all hope to do something worthwhile."

HELEN KELLER

ACTIVIST FOR THE DEAF AND BLIND

Helen Keller was born in 1880 in Alabama. When she was a year and a half old, she became sick with a fever that left her deaf and blind. She could no longer communicate with her parents and often had tantrums as a result of her frustration.

When she was seven, Helen's parents hired a woman named Anne Sullivan to help her. Anne had been blind as a child, but surgery had restored her sight. Anne showed Helen how to spell words by drawing letters onto Helen's palms. Helen didn't understand until one day Anne ran water over one of Helen's hands and spelled out W-A-T-E-R in the other—that's when it finally clicked!

Once Helen mastered this way of communicating, Anne taught her how to read braille, a series of raised bumps that form letters. Helen learned to read by tracing her fingers over the bumps and eventually went on to read French, German, Greek, and Latin, all in braille! When Helen wanted to learn how to talk, her parents hired a teacher who taught Helen to say words by letting her feel the vibrations on the teacher's mouth as the teacher spoke. Soon, Helen was saying letters, words, and, finally, complete sentences.

At sixteen, Helen enrolled in school for the first time. Anne stayed by her side during classes and signed into her hand. Helen graduated with honors and was accepted into Radcliffe College, the women's branch of Harvard. At college, she wrote about her unique experiences, and her work was published in magazines. She also wrote two books, *The Story of My Life* and *The World I Live In*. As Helen grew older, she made it her life's mission to help other deaf and blind people. She and Anne traveled the world giving speeches and raising money for the American Foundation for the Blind.

For her work, Helen was honored with many awards, including the Presidential Medal of Freedom, the highest award a US citizen can receive. She died at the age of eighty-eight, but her story of perseverance will live on forever.

1991–

"If I had the attention of the world for five minutes, I would ask everyone to think about how much they have. In Canada we have so much stuff. I'd ask people to think about what they want and what they really need. I'd ask them to share just a little bit no matter where they lived."

RYAN HRELJAC

PHILANTHROPIST

In first grade, Ryan had a pen pal named Jimmy Akana who lived in Uganda. In one of their letters, Jimmy wrote about how hard it was for his community to find water. Ryan had learned about this issue at school. His teacher had explained that in many countries, people have to walk for hours just to drink or bathe. Ryan didn't think it was right that getting water was so hard for some people, while for others, like Ryan and his classmates, a water fountain was just down the hall.

Ryan set off on a mission to build a well in Jimmy's village. He asked his parents for money in exchange for doing chores, but he soon found out that a well costs $2,000—way more than he was able to raise on his own! Still, he refused to give up. He began speaking at clubs, in schools, and any place where people would listen. A year later, Ryan was finally able to raise enough money to purchase a well for Jimmy's village.

After this success, Ryan wanted to do more. He knew that if he could raise money for Jimmy's village, he could find money for others in need, too. That's why in 2001, he helped found Ryan's Well Foundation to provide clean water for people around the world. Within two years, Ryan's Well raised over one million dollars for clean-water projects and built over 120 wells throughout Africa. As of 2018, they have completed 1,166 water projects in sixteen countries and have provided close to 900,000 people with water. Ryan has won many awards for his hard work, including the World of Children Founders' Award and Planet Africa's Nelson Mandela Humanitarian Award.

As a young adult, Ryan continues to spend much of his time speaking about water issues and working for his foundation. As for Jimmy, he moved to Canada in high school to live with Ryan and his family, after his village in Uganda became unsafe. There's no doubt that Ryan and Jimmy will be bonded for life by their shared experiences.

1995–

"Regardless of where you come from, you can go anywhere in the world by reading a book."

ADELE ANN TAYLOR

ADVOCATE FOR LITERACY

Ever since Adele was a young girl growing up in New Jersey, she had a passion for reading. But some of her classmates didn't enjoy reading as much as she did, and others really struggled with it. Adele eventually found out that millions of people all over the world never even have the chance to learn how to read. She also learned that not knowing how to read led to difficulty finding a good job.

Determined to change this, Adele and her parents thought of some ways to encourage others to read. Together, they decided to throw a big holiday party and ask every guest to bring a book to donate. That night, Adele collected over two hundred books! In 2008, she started Adele's Literacy Library (ALL) to continue fostering a love of learning and books. She was thirteen years old. As part of her organization, she collected books and donated them to schools and libraries. Read ALL You Can, one of the many programs that Adele started, was used in some elementary schools to get kids excited about reading. The purpose of it was to challenge students to read as many books as they could in a month. Adele also created an ALL Ambassadors program to teach kids how to spread a love of books in their own communities.

Today, Adele's organization has donated hundreds of thousands of books to those in need. One of Adele's main focuses as a young adult is to raise money for college scholarships so that kids whose families can't afford college are still able to go. She has partnered with big companies like Target and Build-A-Bear Workshop to get her message out.

Her hard work has given her a lot of recognition. In 2009, she was named Miss Heartland's Outstanding Teen. She's also received the HALO Award from Nickelodeon and the Black Girls Rock! Award from BET. She has big ideas for her future, too; she wants to become a lawyer and also plans to write her own book someday.

1993-

AKRIT JASWAL

SURGEON

In the year 2000, the parents of an eight-year-old girl in India heard about a child surgeon who might be able to help them. Their daughter's fingers were stuck together after a terrible burn, and they had been looking for a surgeon. The family was too poor to pay for a hospital visit, so they contacted a seven-year-old kid named Akrit. He was their last hope. Akrit performed the operation and successfully separated the girl's fingers. This made him the youngest person to perform surgery in the modern history of the world.

Akrit's parents knew that he had a special gift when he was a baby. By ten months old, he could walk and talk. By the age of two, he was reading and writing. At five years old, Akrit had learned to read English, which was a second language for him. Not only was he reading English, but he was also reading very advanced texts, including Shakespeare!

By the time Akrit was six, he knew he wanted to study medicine. He saw poor people in India who couldn't afford medical treatment and made it his mission to help them. When the doctors in his hometown found out that he wanted to study science and medicine, they invited him to watch them operate on patients. Soon, news of this spread, and people began coming to Akrit for medical advice and treatment. It was then that he performed the surgery on the little girl's fingers.

Akrit knew he needed a good education, so he enrolled in college at age eleven, which made him the youngest university student in all of India. He was even invited to London to discuss his ideas about curing cancer with other scientists. The scientists thought Akrit had some interesting theories, but it was clear that he needed to learn more before he could begin his research. That's exactly what Akrit is doing now. He spends his time learning about medicine and continues pursuing his dreams of helping others.

1991–

"When you educate a child . . .
you're educating the future."

THANDIWE CHAMA

CHILDREN'S RIGHTS ACTIVIST

When Thandiwe Chama was eight years old, her school in Zambia shut down because there were not enough teachers. There were no other schools nearby that would accept students. Thandiwe was upset by this, so she gathered sixty of her classmates and led them on a walk to find another school. She refused to give up, demanding her right to an education. Eventually, the students were allowed to attend another school, and ever since then, Thandiwe has been fighting for children's rights.

Following this victory, Thandiwe began to fight for the right to learn inside of a covered building instead of outside in the sun. This is very important in Zambia, where temperatures can reach a scorching 104 degrees Fahrenheit. Thandiwe asked the government for money to construct this building, and after the government agreed, she asked for more money to buy land to add more classrooms.

The Zambian government eventually presented Thandiwe with an award and invited her to speak. She used this opportunity to talk about the rights of children in her country. She believes that every single child has a right to an education, no matter how poor they are.

Not only is Thandiwe passionate about education; she also helped support the rights of people who have AIDS, a disease that has killed over two million people in Africa. Thandiwe knew that education was the best way to stop the spread of AIDS, which is why she even wrote a book on this topic to help spread information and awareness.

Thandiwe's hard work was recognized in 2007, when, at age sixteen, she won the International Children's Peace Prize. Shortly after, a library was donated to Thandiwe's elementary school in her honor. Thandiwe's goal is to make sure everybody knows that when children are educated, they will be better prepared to fight for change—not just in Zambia but around the world.

1961–

"I think kids are attracted to success."

NADIA COMĂNECI

ATHLETE

At the 1976 Olympics in Montreal, Canada, fourteen-year-old Nadia Comăneci became the first person in history to score a perfect ten in gymnastics! By the time the Olympics were over, this young gymnast from Romania had captured the world's attention by earning seven perfect tens, three gold medals, one bronze medal, and one silver medal.

Nadia first signed up for gymnastics when she was in kindergarten. Not long after, a famous gymnastics coach came to her school looking for kids to join his team. He saw Nadia perform and thought she'd be perfect. As part of the team, Nadia practiced two to three hours each day. She fell down a lot during practice, but she always got back up.

At seven years old, she began competing. At the Romanian Nationals, she came in at a disappointing thirteenth place. A year later, she competed again in the same event and won first place, making her the youngest gymnast ever to win that competition! At the age of twelve, she went to live in a training school where she trained eight hours a day, six days a week in hope of making it to the Olympics.

Nadia's performance at the 1976 Summer Olympics changed the way the world viewed female athletes. Her wins made her the youngest all-around Olympic gold medalist in history. She proved that girls could be just as competitive and athletic as boys. She also brought attention to gymnastics, making it more popular than ever. Girls all over the world looked up to her. At the next Olympic Games, Nadia won two more gold medals and two silvers. In 1993, at age nineteen, Nadia retired and was inducted into the International Gymnastics Hall of Fame. Three years after that, she was honored as one of the 100 Most Important Women of the Twentieth Century. She moved to the United States in 1989 and eventually became a US citizen.

Today, Nadia owns a gymnastics academy along with other businesses, and she supports many charities. Her achievements will go down in history, and she will always be remembered as a true Olympic legend.

1596–1617

POCAHONTAS

PEACEMAKER

Born into the Powhatan tribe more than four hundred years ago, Pocahontas was the daughter of a powerful chief. When she was twelve, English settlers arrived near Powhatan land and built a settlement called Jamestown. Sometimes the Powhatans traded goods and got along with the settlers—but other times they had disagreements that turned violent. On one of these occasions, Chief Powhatan's warriors captured the English leader, Captain John Smith, and planned to have him killed. Just as Smith was about to be executed, Pocahontas jumped into action, placing her head on top of Smith's. She begged her father to spare the captain's life and let him go. Lucky for Smith, the chief agreed to Pocahontas's request.

After this ordeal, the Powhatans and the settlers became much friendlier with one another. They began trading regularly, and Pocahontas sometimes brought food to the settlers, saving them from starvation. Then, one day, Captain Smith had to return home to England. Without the captain, the relationship between the tribe and the English became tense once again.

A few years later, at the age of eighteen, Pocahontas was captured by the new English captain, Samuel Argall. He agreed to release her in exchange for English prisoners that her father was holding captive. While the men negotiated the deal, Pocahontas fell in love with a tobacco farmer named John Rolfe. Her father eventually came to an agreement with Argall, but Pocahontas decided to stay with the English to be with Rolfe. A year later, she and Rolfe got married and had a baby. During this time, Pocahontas once again helped keep the relationship between the English and the Powhatans peaceful.

A little while later, Pocahontas sailed back to England with Rolfe and changed her name to Rebecca. She had planned to return to Virginia but became very ill and died at age twenty-three. She will always be remembered as a brave peacemaker and an important figure in American history.

1940–

"Success is no accident. It is hard work, perseverance, learning, studying, sacrifice."

PELÉ

ATHLETE

Growing up in a poor village in Brazil, Edson Arantes do Nascimento and his friends spent their free time playing football (known in the United States as soccer). Edson was so good that his friends nicknamed him Pelé after his favorite soccer player, whose name was Bile. They didn't know at the time that they were pronouncing Bile's name wrong, but the name stuck, and Edson has kept it ever since.

When Pelé was eleven, he played for a local soccer club. His coach took notice of Pelé's talent and introduced him to the directors of Brazil's professional team, the Santos, declaring that Pelé would one day be the best soccer player in the world. Pelé kept practicing, and four years later, at the age of fifteen, he signed with the Santos.

Pelé had a winning combination of speed, balance, and the ability to control the ball. He also had a powerful shot and was incredibly skilled at passing. At sixteen, he scored his first international goal against Argentina, making him the youngest soccer player in history to score in an international game. The year after that, he scored a whopping fifty-eight goals in a season—a record that's unmatched to this day! When he was seventeen, Pele helped his team win the 1958 World Cup. He set three World Cup records that day: He was the youngest to score a goal, the youngest to score a hat trick (three goals in one game), and the youngest to play in a World Cup Final.

Pelé played his last World Cup at the age of thirty. He scored fourteen out of nineteen goals and brought home the trophy for Brazil. He retired at thirty-four, but two years later, the New York Cosmos offered him a multimillion dollar contract to get back in the game. On October 1, 1977, at thirty-seven years old, the soccer legend played his last game, and it just so happened that the Cosmos were playing his old team—the Santos! Pelé decided to play the first half for the Cosmos and the second half for the Santos. His very last goal was a free kick for the Cosmos, who won the game two to one. In 1999, Pelé was voted the Football Player of the Century. Like his coach predicted, Pelé had become the best soccer player in the world!

1412–1431

"I am not afraid; I was born to do this."

JOAN of ARC

WARRIOR

Legend has it that when Joan of Arc was a small child, an angel came to her in a vision. The angel told her she would lead the French to victory in a battle against the English. At the age of sixteen, Joan decided it was time to fulfill her destiny.

At the time, England and France were fighting the Hundred Years' War. After King Charles IV of France died in 1328 without a son to take his place, England seized the opportunity to take over France.

Joan asked a local commander to take her to Charles VII, the rightful successor to the French throne. The commander laughed at her, thinking she was just a poor farm girl. Joan rallied support from other leaders, and soon the commander had to grant Joan her wish. Joan cut her hair, practiced combat, and put on knight's armor before setting out on her quest.

Joan asked Charles VII for an army. He didn't take her seriously at first, but after she told him that this was God's will, he gave her what she wanted. Joan and her army captured one fortress and then another. When she arrived in the city of Orléans, the French people greeted her with cheers. They had heard of Joan's visions and had faith that she would save them from British oppression. Joan was a fierce warrior, never giving up, even when she was struck in the neck by an arrow. With Joan in charge, the French army fought off the English and forced them to retreat. Charles VII was crowned the king of France after Joan reclaimed the city of Reims.

Joan fulfilled her vision but continued to fight and was eventually taken captive by the British, who put her on trial for witchcraft. She was burned alive at the stake at the age of nineteen. Before she died, she prayed and forgave her enemies. In 1920, the Catholic Church made Joan the patron saint of France and soldiers. Joan lived a short life, but almost six hundred years later, we still remember her courage.

1901–1971

"The trumpet . . . just know that if it plays right, it's going to be appreciated in any language."

LOUIS ARMSTRONG

MUSICIAN

The New Orleans neighborhood that young Louis Armstrong grew up in was so tough, it was nicknamed "the battleground." As a child, Louis (pronounced *loo*-ee) spent a lot of time on his own, and one of his favorite things to do was watch the local jazz musicians perform. When Louis was in fifth grade, he dropped out of school to work. Eventually, he saved enough money to buy himself a cornet, which is a type of horn instrument. Because he couldn't afford lessons, he taught himself to play.

At the age of twelve, Louis was sent to a home for troubled kids. There he joined a band and learned to read music. By the time he was a teenager, he was an excellent horn player. He met a jazz musician named Joe "King" Oliver, one of the best cornetists in New Orleans. Joe taught Louis everything he knew, and by the time Louis was seventeen, he had taken Joe's place in Kid Ory's band, the most popular band in the region. This success allowed Louis to quit his other jobs and focus on music. He began playing at parties, dances, funerals, and honky-tonks (small bars that host music). The summer he turned eighteen, Louis was performing in bands on riverboats on the Mississippi River. It wasn't long before Joe invited Louis to join his band in Chicago, where the two started making records together.

A rising star, Louis traveled to New York City, where he switched from the cornet to the trumpet. He later moved back to Chicago to form his own band. That's when Louis began singing. His voice had a unique rough sound, and people couldn't get enough of it. Louis began traveling around the world, singing and playing the trumpet for eager audiences. Some of his biggest hits include "What a Wonderful World" and "Hello, Dolly!"

Louis died at the age of sixty-nine but will forever be remembered as one of the greatest jazz musicians of all time. Today, you can visit the Louis Armstrong House in Queens, New York, to find out more about his life.

1838–1914

MARGARET KNIGHT

INVENTOR

Growing up in New Hampshire during the Industrial Revolution, Margaret Knight began working in a cotton mill at the age of twelve. One day, a loom malfunctioned and a piece flew off. Margaret watched as it struck another worker, injuring him badly. That day, Margaret came up with an idea for a device that could automatically shut off a machine when it malfunctioned.

She got to work on her new invention, and after a few weeks she brought it to her bosses, who began using it right away. It reduced the number of deaths and injuries to workers almost immediately. News of her invention spread, and cotton mills throughout the country adopted the device. Unfortunately, because Margaret was so young, she didn't get paid for her invention.

When Margaret was an adult, she moved to Massachusetts and took a job at a company that produced paper bags. At that time, paper bags were narrow and flimsy. Margaret wanted to invent a machine that could make a sturdy bag with a flat bottom. It took two years, but she finally built a wooden model of her machine that could cut, fold, and glue bags by turning a crank. While she was in Boston making her model into an actual iron machine, a man saw her invention and stole her idea! During that time, many people thought women couldn't be inventors, but Margaret wasn't about to let someone steal her hard work. She filed a lawsuit against the man and won. Soon people all over the world began using Margaret's new and improved paper bag. You might still carry your lunch in this kind of bag today!

Margaret's inventions earned her the nickname "Lady Edison," after the famous inventor Thomas Edison. Some of her more popular creations include machines to cut and sew shoes; the barbecue spit; a reel for sewing machines; and the rotary engine. She invented over ninety products in her lifetime. If you're ever in Washington, DC, check out her original bag-making machine at the Smithsonian's National Museum of American History.

1997-

"The big message is to inspire others and go out there and change the world."

JACK ANDRAKA

SCIENTIST

After losing a family friend to pancreatic cancer, fourteen-year-old Jack Andraka was driven to find a way to fight this disease. He began doing experiments in a small laboratory in his basement. What he discovered would set off an amazing series of events.

Jack learned that the reason many people die of pancreatic cancer is because they often don't know they have it until it's too late. His research told him that as the cancer grows, it sends off a quiet signal. One day in science class, Jack came up with the idea for a sensor that could detect this signal. All it would require is a few drops of blood from the patient.

Jack needed to find a lab that would work with him on his sensor, so he sent out two hundred e-mails to labs around the country. He only got one response back, from Dr. Maitra at Johns Hopkins School of Medicine. Dr. Maitra invited Jack to his lab, where Jack began working every day after school and most weekends well into the night. He even spent his fifteenth birthday in the lab. It wasn't easy. Jack didn't know what most of the equipment was, and he had a few mishaps, but early one morning, Jack found that his test had detected the signal! Jack's test only costs three cents to make and takes just five minutes to complete. It's also 90 percent accurate. This means it has the potential to change the outcome of cancer for millions of people! Since that day, Jack has expanded the test to detect two other types of cancers.

Jack won the $75,000 grand prize at the Intel International Science and Engineering Fair, making him an instant celebrity in his hometown of Crownsville, Maryland. In 2014, he won the Jefferson Award, the nation's most important award for public service. The test is still in its early stages, and it will take years before doctors are allowed to use it on their patients, but Jack's contribution was a huge step forward in cancer research.

1999–

"I believe that youth have the power to do incredible things."

KATIE STAGLIANO

PHILANTHROPIST

When Katie Stagliano was nine years old, she brought home a cabbage seedling as part of a school project. She planted the seed in the corner of her yard and watered it every day. Katie's cabbage grew and grew—and didn't stop growing until it reached forty pounds! Katie wanted to do something special with her cabbage, so she donated it to a soup kitchen, where it helped feed over 275 hungry people! This inspired Katie to do even more to help those in need.

Katie came up with the idea to plant gardens across the country and then donate the harvest to feed hungry people. She named her foundation Katie's Krops. Her school donated land for the garden, and her classmates helped pick the vegetables and distribute them.

When Katie was twelve, the local soup kitchen where she had donated her first cabbage was forced to shut its doors. The people who depended on it now had nowhere to eat, so Katie decided to expand her project to include Katie's Krops Dinners. She gathered a group of volunteers in her South Carolina neighborhood who promised not only to grow gardens but also to prepare meals and serve dinners. Once a month, these volunteers gather vegetables from their garden. Then, with the help of a trained chef, they prepare meals for those in need. In 2016, this group served 2,347 meals at twelve dinners.

Katie's foundation also recently started a free camp for kids who want to travel to South Carolina to work on a farm. At the camp, the kids can learn growing techniques, host a project, and find out about food safety.

Now Katie's Krops has one hundred gardens in thirty-three states and donates thousands of pounds of produce to help feed the hungry. All of these gardens are managed by kids ages nine to sixteen. One of Katie's goals is to empower other kids to start their own vegetable gardens. She hopes to end hunger, one vegetable at a time.

1996–

"One of my intentions with *Rookie* is for the girls reading it to know that they are already cool enough and smart enough and pretty enough."

TAVI GEVINSON

FASHION ICON

Ever since Tavi Gevinson was a young girl growing up in Chicago, she spent her free time cutting out photos from fashion magazines and pasting them into a binder. One day, when Tavi was twelve, she went to her friend's house for a sleepover. Her friend's sister showed her a fashion blog online. Tavi was inspired and decided to start writing her own blog, called *StyleRookie*.

When Tavi first started blogging, she wanted to learn everything she could about fashion. She began looking at old magazines and fashion campaigns from as far back as the 1980s. Then she decided to break all the rules of fashion. She wore tops as skirts and even made a coat hanger into a necklace. Part of what made Tavi so popular is that she wasn't afraid to look different.

It's not easy to gain followers when you're new to blogging, but Tavi had a unique sense of style. She wrote funny articles and offered great advice. *StyleRookie* was so thoughtful and interesting that people began to think the content was written by an adult. They couldn't believe that a young girl could be so intelligent and creative. Soon, thirty thousand people a day were reading *StyleRookie*!

It wasn't long before the fashion industry took notice. Famous designers wanted to get to know Tavi, and in 2010, at the age of fourteen, she was invited to the Dior spring fashion show in Paris. Another designer flew her to Tokyo to be the guest of honor at a fashion event. Designers began sending her outfits in hopes that she would write about them on her blog. A famous magazine called *Harper's Bazaar* even asked her to write a review of their spring collection.

When Tavi turned fifteen, she shifted her focus away from fashion and created *Rookie* magazine online. This pop culture magazine covers important topics that affect teenage girls. In 2014, Tavi was named one of the 25 Most Influential Teens by *Time* magazine. She continues to be a major influence on young people today.

1996–

KELVIN DOE

In his home in Sierra Leone, Africa, thirteen-year-old Kelvin would rummage through garbage and collect old electronics that had been cast aside. He'd dump them out on the living room floor and take apart the pieces to see how they worked.

The area where Kelvin lived in Africa was so poor that the community only had electricity once a week. Kelvin wanted to be able to study at night, so he invented a battery by mixing ingredients in a tin cup. Next, he built a generator to power the electricity for his home. He took a chance and entered his generator into a competition. Kelvin became a finalist in the competition and was chosen to go to a three-day summer innovation camp.

The purpose of this camp was to help kids find ways to solve tough problems in their community. Kelvin had always wanted to build a radio station to bring people together to discuss important issues. So that's exactly what he did! He took an FM radio, an amplifier, and a transmitter and began his very own radio station. It was an instant success! By age sixteen, Kelvin was hiring other kids to help him run the station and bring music and talk shows to people in his community. The average age of his employees was twelve.

Kelvin's work earned him an invitation to the United States, where he attended a program that allowed him to use labs and do research at the Massachusetts Institute of Technology, or MIT. While he was in the United States, Kelvin also gave talks to college engineering students at MIT and Harvard University. His work brought him so much attention that when he returned home, the president of Sierra Leone awarded him the Presidential Gold Medal!

These days, Kelvin is considered one of the most respected inventors in Africa, and has been invited to meet with leaders around the world. Kelvin stays busy running his new company called KDoe-Tech. He's always working on new inventions to help improve the lives of others.

2005–

"Frustration is fuel that can lead to the development of an innovative and useful idea."

MARLEY DIAS

ADVOCATE FOR DIVERSITY

Eleven-year-old Marley Dias loved to read—but every time she picked up a book in her New Jersey school, she felt disappointed. All the books were about white boys and their experiences. She wished her teacher would assign a book that featured a black girl as the main character.

One day, Marley told her mom about her frustration, and her mom asked her what she was going to do about it. Marley knew then that if she wanted things to change, she would have to change them herself. She came up with the idea to collect one thousand books that featured a black girl as the main character. That's how her campaign #1000BlackGirlBooks was born.

Marley didn't collect one thousand books. . . . She has collected over eleven thousand total since the start of her campaign! With her success, she set up a black girl book club at school. She also began speaking out about her cause and spreading the message that the world needs more books featuring diverse characters. This way, *all* children can know that their stories are important.

News of Marley's work spread quickly. Newspapers and magazines began calling for interviews, and she was even invited to be a guest on the television show *Ellen*. The more people heard about her campaign, the more donations she received.

The year Marley turned twelve, she got her very own book deal with Scholastic. Not only was she collecting books; she now had the chance to write one! Her book is about the success of her campaign and how every child has the ability to make their own dreams come true. In 2017, Marley attended the Forbes Women's Summit in New York City, an event that celebrates incredible girls and women around the world. At the event, she discussed how the lack of diversity in books hurts everyone—and how she was able to turn something that upset her into a movement toward positivity and progress.

1943-2008

BOBBY FISCHER

CHESS CHAMPION

When Bobby Fischer was six years old, his sister brought home a chess set from a candy store in Brooklyn where they lived. Bobby found the game interesting and taught himself how to play by reading the booklet that came with the set. By the time he was eight, he needed more people to play with, so he asked his mom to put an ad in the paper. The chess writer for the local newspaper invited Bobby to attend a chess exhibition, where talented players would be competing. Bobby played at the exhibition, and afterward, the head of the Brooklyn Chess Club invited him to become a member.

By the age of twelve, Bobby was competing against adults in the Manhattan Chess Club. His opponents gave him nicknames like "The Boy Robot," because he hardly ever made mistakes, and "The Corduroy Killer," because he always wore corduroy pants. One of the reasons Bobby was so good was because he read every book he could find about chess. He studied different moves and strategies, and he never lost focus while playing the game.

When Bobby was thirteen, he made history by becoming the youngest US Junior Chess Champion ever. Not long after, he played a renowned chess player named Donald Byrne. Bobby made a bold move and sacrificed his queen—but ended up winning the game! It was such a nail-biting competition that some called it the game of the century.

A year later, Bobby won another competition called the United States Open Chess Championship. By the time he was fifteen, he was the international grand-master chess champion, making him the youngest person to win this honor. Over the next few years, he continued to win victories around the world. He won the World Chess Championship in 1972 and held on to that title for three years.

Bobby Fischer spent his later years living in Iceland, where he died at the age of sixty-four. He brought attention to a game that most people knew very little about, making it as competitive and thrilling as any other sport.

1997–

"You must not treat others with cruelty . . . you must fight others but through peace and through dialogue and through education."

MALALA YOUSAFZAI
ACTIVIST FOR GIRLS' RIGHTS AND EDUCATION

As a young girl, Malala Yousafzai had a peaceful life growing up in the Swat Valley of Pakistan. That all changed in 2007 when a group called the Taliban took over the region. The Taliban changed the laws and told girls they were no longer allowed to attend school. Malala had dreams of one day becoming a doctor, a teacher, or a politician. She knew that an education could secure her future, and she wasn't about to let anyone take that right away from her.

When Malala was eleven, she spoke out about this injustice for the first time in public. A year later, with her father's support, she began writing a blog called *Diary of a Pakistani Schoolgirl* for the BBC, an international news organization. People around the world began paying attention to her story.

Once the Pakistani government regained control of the region, Malala was finally allowed to go back to school—but the Taliban were still causing problems. They threatened to kill Malala if she didn't stop opposing them. One day, members of the Taliban boarded Malala's school bus and shot her in the head. Malala survived, miraculously, and moved to England to have multiple surgeries. Six months later, she began attending school there. Getting shot only made Malala more passionate about her cause. She gave a speech in front of the United Nations about the need for girls around the world to receive an education. In her speech, she explained that she didn't want revenge for what had happened to her. All she wanted was peace and equal opportunities for all people.

In 2014, at age sixteen, Malala became the youngest person ever to win the Nobel Peace Prize. She wrote a book about her experiences, titled *I Am Malala*, and today she continues to advocate for girls to go to school. Her work has become so important that the United Nations recently named July 12, Malala's birthday, "World Malala Day." This is a day to spread awareness about the educational rights of girls everywhere.

1881–1973

"Art begins with the individual."

PABLO PICASSO

ARTIST

Pablo Picasso was seven years old when his father, an art teacher, began giving him lessons. When he was nine, Pablo finished his first painting, called *Le Picador*. It was a painting of a man on a horse during a bullfight. Pablo would go on to paint many more horse scenes like it in his long career as an artist.

Pablo loved art, but he didn't like school and was often in trouble. When he disrupted the class, his teachers would send him to a small cell with white walls and a single hard bench. The teachers considered this punishment, but Pablo loved this time alone. He sat on that bench for hours with a sketchpad and a pencil, making art without any interruptions. When Pablo was sixteen, his father enrolled him in the best art academy in Spain. But even at this school, Pablo took no interest in his work and stopped attending his classes. Instead, he spent his time going to art museums to see famous paintings.

Pablo didn't want to paint the way other artists painted. He wanted to do something that had never been done before. In 1900, when Pablo was nineteen, he traveled to Paris and became friends with other artists. Pablo's early paintings were real-life scenes of people and events, but soon he began experimenting with different types of art. He and another artist named George Braque invented an art form called *cubism*, where many different points of views can be captured in one painting. (For example, a painting that shows both the front and side of a face.)

Throughout his life, Picasso made over fifty thousand pieces of art, creating oil paintings, sculptures, drawings, collages, and rugs. He also wrote plays and poetry. In 2015, his painting called *The Women of Algiers* sold for $180 million, making it one of the most expensive pieces of art ever sold.

Picasso died in 1973 at the age of ninety-one. His art can be found in museums around the world.

1936–

SYLVIA MENDEZ

ACTIVIST FOR RACIAL EQUALITY

When Sylvia was nine years old, her aunt tried to enroll her, her brother, and her cousins in the same neighborhood school in Westminster, California. The school told Sylvia's aunt that while her own children could attend because they had light-colored eyes and skin, Sylvia and her brother could not because they had dark skin and a Mexican last name. Her aunt stormed out of the office, refusing to enroll any of the children.

During the 1940s, separating children based on their race was legal. According to this practice, Sylvia and her brother would have to go to a Hispanic school ten blocks away from the all-white school. The Hispanic school was a tiny wooden shack with only two rooms, while the all-white school was a beautiful brick building with a large playground surrounded by trees. Sylvia's parents knew that if their children were going to get a good education, they would have to find a way to attend the all-white school. So they decided to fight back. They, along with four other Hispanic families, hired a lawyer to sue four school districts in California. The case became known as *Mendez versus Westminster*.

Sylvia went to court every day to watch the trial. The case lasted for two months. On March 18, 1946, the judge ruled that segregation was an unfair practice. The Hispanic families won their lawsuit, making California the first state in the country to end segregation based on skin color.

Sylvia Mendez was finally allowed to get the education she deserved. After studying hard and graduating from high school, she went on to become a nurse. When she retired, she began speaking out and educating others about her experience while encouraging students to stay in school. In 2011, President Barack Obama awarded Sylvia the Congressional Medal of Freedom for her activism.

1995–

RENE SILVA

JOURNALIST

One Saturday afternoon, seventeen-year-old Rene Silva's community became caught in a police standoff with drug dealers. Rene lived in a poor neighborhood in Brazil known for its high crime rate. During the standoff, reporters couldn't get into the neighborhood to find out what was going on. Rene and his friends began posting updates on social media to let the world know how dangerous the situation had become. His quick thinking during the crisis impressed the world, and by the next evening he had twenty thousand followers on social media. Rene became an overnight celebrity, but he didn't stumble upon this success accidentally. He was prepared to cover this story from his years of experience reporting.

When Rene Silva was eleven years old, his teacher asked him to write a newspaper about problems in his community. He created a newspaper called *Voz da Comunidade*, meaning "The Voice of the Community." Rene was the reporter, the photographer, the printer, and the sales manager. The first few printings of the newspaper were done using the school's old copy machine. As more people heard about his work, local businesses began putting advertisements in his paper. Rene spent the money he made from the advertisers to make more copies. Soon he was handing out over five thousand copies of his newspaper to people in his community.

The newspaper continued to do well, and by the time Rene was fourteen, he could afford to buy computers and a webcam to stream news live (as it was happening). He asked his friends to help him out, and soon he had a whole staff made up of kids. Rene wanted to reach even more people, so he eventually put the newspaper on the Internet. Once, during a bad rainstorm, he reported about people who were trapped in a mudslide. With his help, officials were able to find the victims and bring them to a shelter.

Today, Rene's website has a huge following of people from around the world and is still growing. Rene believes that if you have a good education along with access to technology, you can achieve anything.

1989–

MICHELLE WIE

ATHLETE

Growing up in Hawaii, Michelle Wie enjoyed listening to music, hanging out with friends, and working hard in school. But when she wasn't doing those things, she was playing golf. Her father was her coach, and her mom, who had been an amateur golf champion in South Korea, provided encouragement and support. By the time Michelle was ten years old, she had qualified for a United States Golf Association (USGA) tournament.

At the age of thirteen, Michelle became the youngest player in history to win a USGA event for adults. The following year, she became the fourth woman and the youngest person ever to compete against men in a Professional Golf Association Tour event. There was no doubt about it—at such a young age, Michelle was already a world-class golfer!

At the age of sixteen, Michelle decided it was time to go pro. She signed a contract with Nike and Sony for over ten million dollars per year. At a height of six foot one, her powerful game earned her the nickname "Big Wiesy." Fans adored her, and she quickly became known for her perfect swing. She could hit a golf ball fifty yards farther than the average professional female golfer!

It wasn't long before her career really took off. In 2005, Michelle became the first female golfer to qualify for a USGA National Men's tournament. She was a tough competitor, and she often intimidated much older players. Unfortunately, by the time she was eighteen, Michelle began suffering from wrist injuries that affected her game. She hit a major slump but was determined to continue playing. It was a good thing she never thought about giving up, because in 2014 she won the US Women's Open. That's one of the biggest golf tournaments in the US!

Now an adult, Michelle continues to compete. She credits her parents for inspiring her to work hard and follow her dreams.

1998–

"I had a moral obligation to help those kids so that every homeless kid could have equal opportunities."

NICHOLAS LOWINGER

PHILANTHROPIST

Nicholas Lowinger's mother took him to a homeless shelter to volunteer when he was five years old. He met kids just like him—except these kids didn't have proper shoes. Some of their shoes were so old, they were duct-taped together. Nicholas knew that torn shoes made it harder to run, play, or simply get around. That day, Nicholas went home and donated all his shoes that no longer fit.

When Nicholas was twelve, he decided to do a community service project for his upcoming bar mitzvah, a Jewish coming-of-age tradition. He came up with the idea of starting a foundation called Gotta Have Sole to provide brand-new shoes for homeless children.

He started donating to the local homeless shelter in Rhode Island, where he lived. People in his community volunteered by donating new shoes, fundraising, and finding the right shoe sizes for kids in need. Local high schools even began opening Gotta Have Sole clubs to raise funds for the program. This was great, but Nicholas wanted every homeless child in *every* state to have brand-new shoes, so he wrote letters to companies across the country asking them to donate money and shoes to his charity. He also spoke to large audiences and the heads of big corporations about his cause. They responded by providing thousands of pairs of shoes and donating money. News of Nicholas's work spread, and homeless shelters across the country began reaching out to him for help.

Since beginning his charity in 2010, Gotta Have Sole has donated over forty-five thousand pairs of shoes in forty-three states. Nicholas's goal is to put new shoes on the feet of as many children in homeless shelters across the country as possible. He knows that this will help kids feel confident and allow them to have more opportunities.

Nicholas hopes his work will inspire other kids to make a difference in the world. He is proof that one little idea can grow into a huge project that can improve the lives of others.

2001–

AUTUMN DE FOREST

ARTIST

One day, Autumn de Forest's father was staining wood in his garage when Autumn asked if she could help. He gave her a paintbrush and a piece of plywood and went back to work. Next thing he knew, Autumn had created a beautiful painting. This painting looked like the work of a professional artist. Autumn's parents knew their daughter had a special gift, so they bought her supplies and built an art studio for her. It paid off, because by the time Autumn was seven years old, her paintings were selling for thousands of dollars.

At nine years old, Autumn started being homeschooled instead of going to traditional school so she could focus on painting. By age eleven, she had signed up to show her work with Park West Gallery, one of the biggest art dealers in the US.

In 2014, when Autumn was thirteen, Disney asked her to create a series of princess paintings. The following year, she traveled to Rome to receive an award from the Vatican. This special award is given to people under thirty-five who have shown amazing talent. While at the Vatican, she saw the pope and gave him one of her paintings! Two years later, the Butler Institute of American Art offered to exhibit her work. This made her the youngest artist in history to have an exhibit at a major museum. Autumn has even been to the White House. First Lady Michelle Obama invited her to be a mentor to other young artists.

Unlike many other artists, Autumn doesn't have one style of painting; she paints what feels right to her, whether that's scenery, animals in nature, portraits, or abstract art. Autumn loves painting, but she also loves giving back to her community. That's why she donates some of the money she's made to charities and volunteers at her local church in Las Vegas. She also speaks out about the importance of keeping art in schools.

Today, Autumn's work is exhibited all over the world and hangs in galleries next to famous artists like Picasso. She has sold over seven million dollars' worth of art. She continues to inspire people with her creativity and self-expression.

1972-

❯❯ MICHAEL CHANG ❮❮

ATHLETE

Michael Chang has set many youngest-player records in tennis. He was the youngest player to win the US Open, the youngest to reach the semifinals, and the youngest to win a Grand Slam at the French Open. He was also the youngest to be ranked in the top five tennis players in the world!

By the time Michael was seven years old, it was clear that he had serious talent. His parents always told him that he should do what he enjoys, and if that meant playing tennis, they were happy to help him pursue his dream. The whole family pitched in. His brother became his coach, his mom quit her job as a chemist to travel with him full-time, and his father managed all the money Michael won from competing.

At twelve years old, Michael was competing in junior tournaments. He did so well that when he was fifteen, Michael dropped out of school to play professionally. He was shorter than his opponents and most of them weighed about twenty pounds more than he did, but he refused to be intimidated. It just made him want to win even more.

In 1987, Michael won the US Open, and two years later, at the age of seventeen, he won the French Open. Not only was he the youngest man to ever win, he was also the first American to win the French Open in the thirty-four years that it had been established. His final opponent, Ivan Lendl, was previously ranked the number-one tennis player in the world.

By 2002, at age thirty, Michael had won thirty-two titles. He retired a year later, having earned over nineteen million dollars. In 2008, he was inducted into the International Tennis Hall of Fame. Now Michael uses all the knowledge and skills he gained over his career to coach other tennis players.

1972–1985

"If we could be friends by just getting to know each other better,
then what are our countries really arguing about?"

SAMANTHA SMITH

US AMBASSADOR

In the fall of 1982, ten-year-old Samantha Smith asked her mother if the United States was planning to go to war with the Soviet Union. The two countries weren't getting along, and Samantha was afraid that they would use deadly weapons to hurt each other. Her mother showed her an article in *Time* magazine explaining that people in both countries shared Samantha's concerns. On the cover of the magazine was a picture of Yuri Andropov, the leader of the Soviet Union. Samantha decided to write to him to find out more about the issue and to express her fears.

A few months after she mailed her letter, she received a phone call from a reporter saying that her letter had been published in a Soviet newspaper, but Samantha wanted to hear back from Andropov directly. She wrote another letter, this time addressing it to the Soviet Union's ambassador in Washington, DC. A week later, Andropov finally responded! He said that the people of the Soviet Union did *not* want to go to war—they were too busy focusing on things like inventing new technology, writing books, and flying into space. Then he invited Samantha and her family to come for a visit over the summer!

Samantha and her family took Andropov up on his offer to come visit and headed to the city of Moscow. Reporters from around the world filmed her trip. She went swimming with Soviet children and visited important landmarks. The people in the Soviet Union realized Samantha was just like them in many ways. After returning from her trip, she spread a message of peace between the Soviet Union and the United States. She became known around the world as the kid ambassador who helped the two countries learn more about each other.

Unfortunately, Samantha died in a plane crash in 1985 when she was thirteen years old. The new Soviet leader at the time and President Ronald Reagan both reached out to Samantha's mother to let her know that people around the world admired her daughter. The Soviet Union even created a stamp in Samantha's honor and named a mountain after her.

1948–

"Anything you read can influence your work,
so I try to read good stuff."

S. E. HINTON

WRITER

Growing up in Oklahoma in the 1950s, Susan Eloise Hinton dreamed of becoming a cattle rancher and wrote stories about cowboys and horses. When she wasn't writing, she was reading. As she grew older, it became harder for her to find books she liked. Most of the books she found were love stories, but she wanted to read about what it was like to be a teenager. She decided that if she couldn't find a book she liked, she'd have to write one herself.

Susan grabbed a pen and paper and got to work. She took her ideas from real-life events and began writing about two high school gangs. In her book, one gang was called the "Greasers" and the others were called the "Socs." These two groups came from different backgrounds and didn't get along. Susan named her book *The Outsiders*, and focused the story on how hard it can be to fit in. She wrote four drafts but never thought about publishing it. That changed when her friend's mother read the book and told her how good it was. She sent Susan's book to an agent, who then sold it to a major publisher. *The Outsiders* came out in 1967, when Susan was just seventeen years old.

The book was met with mixed reviews. Some people didn't like the book, complaining that they didn't want to read about rebellious young people. But mostly, people loved it. Teenagers across the country could relate to the story. The book quickly sold over four million copies. Susan took the money she made from the sales and enrolled in college.

After the success of *The Outsiders*, S. E. Hinton—Susan's author name—continued to write books, many of which were made into movies. Throughout her lifetime, she's been given many awards to honor her contribution to American literature. *The Outsiders* is still being taught in classrooms across the country today.

1989–2001

"Do all you can with what you have,
in the time you have, in the place you are-."

NKOSI JOHNSON

ACTIVIST FOR KIDS WITH HIV/AIDS

When Nkosi Johnson was born in 1989, he was one of seventy thousand children in South Africa who were HIV positive. HIV, or human immunodeficiency virus, is a serious infection that eventually turns into AIDS, or acquired immunodeficiency syndrome, which is a disease that affects the immune system. Nkosi got the infection from his mother, who passed it to him while she was pregnant.

When Nkosi was eight, his foster-mother Gail tried to enroll him in school. But when parents and teachers found out he was HIV positive, they wouldn't let him attend. Gail fought back, refusing to allow people to discriminate against her son because of his illness. Eventually, Nkosi won the right to go to school.

Gail and Nkosi knew that other children who were HIV positive faced the same issues. They wanted to help educate others about the infection, so they set up workshops for students, parents, and teachers to attend. They continued to raise awareness, and soon it became a policy that all HIV-positive children had the right to go to school.

When Nkosi was eleven, he was invited to speak at a conference in front of ten thousand people. His message was that a child with HIV is the same as any other child. At the end of his speech, he said, "Care for us and accept us—we are all human beings. We are normal. We have hands. We have feet. We can walk, we can talk, we have needs just like everyone else. Don't be afraid of us—we are all the same."

Not long after Nkosi gave this speech, he passed away at the age of twelve. At the time, Nkosi was the longest-surviving child born with HIV in South Africa. Thousands of people attended his funeral, and even the former president of South Africa, Nelson Mandela, spoke of Nkosi's bravery. The organization Nkosi's Haven was created in his honor. This is a place where people who have HIV and AIDS can be given the care they need. Nkosi had a short life, but his fight for HIV and AIDS awareness will never be forgotten.

1989–

PRAVEEN KUMAR GORAKAVI

ENGINEER

Praveen Kumar Gorakavi loves science! As a young boy growing up in India, he spent most of his time learning about technology and researching new inventions.

At thirteen years old, Praveen designed a twenty-thousand-year calendar. He figured it out by using complicated mathematical equations. After that, Praveen doubled his efforts and made a forty-thousand-year calendar. Then he made it available for blind people by using a special system to translate it into braille. The calendar was such an incredible invention, it was put on display in the Singapore Science Center.

Two years later, at the age of fifteen, Praveen decided to use his knowledge of technology to help others. He began working on a low-cost design for an artificial leg that would help amputees (people who are missing limbs) walk better. His artificial leg bends at the knee and ankle, making it much more comfortable and easier to use. Soon Praveen was coming up with so many different inventions that it was hard to keep up! For example, he invented a pen that could write in 256 colors and then later focused on missile technology. He wowed a group of top scientists by proving that wax could be used to help propel rockets.

But still, Praveen's main focus continued to be helping others live longer, healthier lives. In India, millions of people don't have access to healthy food or clean water. Praveen wanted to change this, so he invented a way for people to preserve food for up to three years. He also developed a water-purifying system so people could drink clean water.

Praveen has been honored with over one hundred awards for his inventions. The president of India honored him with Balshree, which is one of the top awards given to children for their creativity. In 2010, he became the youngest person to receive the National Bal Bhawan award from the Indian government for Outstanding Engineer/Scientist. As an adult, Praveen continues to do scientific research and works for a company offering advice about ways to improve technology.

1990–

"I am inviting you to step forward, to be seen, and to ask yourself,

'If not me, who? If not now, when?'"

EMMA WATSON

ACTOR AND ACTIVIST

Growing up in Oxfordshire, England, Emma Watson loved to sing and dance. By the age of seven, her performing arts teachers knew that Emma had a special gift. That's why they suggested she try out for the role of Hermione Granger in a movie based on the bestselling Harry Potter book series. Emma had to go to nine auditions before she was finally chosen for the role. It wasn't until later that she found out that J. K. Rowling, the author of the Harry Potter series, was involved in the films—and she'd wanted Emma to play Hermione all along!

The first Harry Potter movie, *Harry Potter and the Sorcerer's Stone*, was released in 2001 when Emma was eleven years old. It was a huge success! The movie received three Academy Awards, and Emma Watson and her costars Daniel Radcliffe (Harry) and Rupert Grint (Ron) received high praise for their work.

Emma spent the next ten years filming the rest of the Harry Potter series, for a total of eight movies—the last two of which were filmed while she was in college! In 2009, Emma enrolled in Brown University in the US and majored in English literature. She graduated in 2014 and gave a moving speech at the United Nations Headquarters that same year. The speech was about equality between women and men.

Still devoted to her acting career, Emma played Belle in Disney's live-action adaptation of *Beauty and the Beast* in 2017, which broke the box office record for highest-grossing PG-rated film of all time. Today, Emma continues to be outspoken about gender equality and protecting the environment. She's become a huge advocate for sustainable fashion (fashion that's environmentally friendly) and often wears chic clothes made from recycled materials. Not only is Emma an amazing actor, she has become an activist and an icon for young people everywhere.

1998–

"... a simple passion—in my case,
the environment—can go a long way."

CASSANDRA LIN

ENVIRONMENTAL ACTIVIST

When Cassandra Lin was in the fifth grade, her class studied the effects of climate change on the planet. She learned that the biggest cause of global warming is humans consuming too much fuel. People burn a lot of coal and oil, and as a result, the entire world heats up.

Feeling motivated, Cassandra rallied her classmates to form the Junior WIN Team, short for the Westerly Innovations Network, the goal of which was to find ways to help both the community and the environment. The group already knew that one way to slow down global warming was to use alternative energies like biodiesel, and they learned that biodiesel could be made from used cooking oil. After seeing an article about a charity that donated money to help people heat their homes, the group had an idea. What if they turned grease into fuel, which could then be used to help heat these families' homes? They could help people *and* be kind to the environment! That's how Project Turn Grease Into Fuel (TGIF) was born.

Cassandra and her friends partnered with grease collectors, biodiesel refiners, and charities to get their project up and running. They asked town officials to set up grease receptacles so residents could recycle their oil, and they got local restaurants to donate their grease. The project was a huge success! They've offset over two million pounds of carbon monoxide (a gas that contributes to Earth's high temperatures) and have donated over twenty-one thousand gallons of bioheat to charities, which has helped over 210 families stay warm.

The determined ten-year-olds didn't stop there. They wrote and helped introduce a bill in Rhode Island, where they live. The bill, which became law in January 2012, would make all businesses recycle their grease. Since then, the group has continued to be active in their community. Their latest campaign helped rebuild local beaches after a terrible hurricane.

Cassandra believes that kids have the power to make real changes in the world. All they have to do is come up with an idea and follow their passion.

1992–

OM PRAKASH GURJAR

CHILDREN'S RIGHTS ACTIVIST

Growing up in India, Om Prakash Gurjar could not afford to attend school and instead worked alongside his parents, planting crops and raising cattle, to help pay back a debt that they owed. But Om Prakash really wanted an education. When he was eight, a group of activists came to his village to help free him. He was placed in a program that trained and educated child laborers (kids who are forced to work). The school was unlike anything he had ever experienced. There, the children were encouraged to speak up and make their interests heard. Om Prakash was finally beginning to understand that children have rights, too.

Inspired by the school, Om Prakash began speaking out about the challenges children like him faced. He wanted people to know that there are laws protecting children. He also wanted children to know they are allowed to have opinions and make decisions for themselves. While studying at his new school, he found out that a local public school was illegally charging parents money to send their kids to school. Om Prakash spoke to an official and demanded action to stop this. The official agreed to help and took a petition to court. The court made the school return all the money to the parents and allow children to attend at no cost. Om Prakash then began going to villages to help free other child laborers and get them enrolled in school. He would tell his own story and convince other children that they, too, had choices and rights that no one could take away.

Om Prakash knows that there is still a long way to go before all children in India are treated with the respect they deserve. His goal is to continue raising awareness about child laborers while working hard to help them create better lives for themselves. In 2006, at age fourteen, he was awarded the International Children's Peace Prize for his efforts.

1935–1977

"I feel I've got to do my best,
whatever I try."

ELVIS PRESLEY

MUSICIAN

When Elvis Aaron Presley was ten years old, he stood up on a chair at the Mississippi-Alabama Fair and sang a song called "Old Shep." He won fifth place and five dollars' worth of rides. Little did anyone know that a few years later, Elvis would change the world of music forever.

Elvis got a guitar for his eleventh birthday, but his family couldn't afford lessons, so Elvis taught himself how to play by watching others perform. Soon Elvis began singing and playing his guitar in school talent shows. When he entered high school, his parents moved to Memphis, Tennessee. There, Elvis continued to enter contests and became a huge fan of blues, jazz, and gospel music. He got his first taste of fame when he won his school talent show. By this time, he had become such a good guitar player that people all over Memphis began noticing his talent. Elvis never went anywhere without his guitar. He even carried it to school.

In 1953, right after graduating from high school, Elvis went to a music studio to record a song for his mother. The owner liked Elvis's style so much that he asked Elvis to record a few songs with other musicians. During a break, Elvis began dancing around the room and playing an old blues song called "That's All Right." Three days later, Elvis's version of the song was on the radio, and that's when his career took off!

Fans went crazy for Elvis's unique style, which was a combination of gospel and country. He also had dance moves nobody had ever seen before. His very first album went to the top of the charts, and his first hit song was "Heartbreak Hotel." People began calling him the King of Rock 'n' Roll!

Throughout his career, Elvis recorded eighteen number-one hits and starred in over thirty movies. He eventually bought a mansion known as Graceland, where he lived until his death at the age of forty-two. Today, Graceland is a museum you can visit to find out more about the man who is credited for being one of the world's very first rock stars.

2000–

"Equality is what unites our society, and everyone needs to understand that not only do we all deserve to be loved, but we deserve to love ourselves for who we are–."

JAZZ JENNINGS

TRANSGENDER ADVOCATE

Jazz Jennings was born a boy, but by the age of two, she knew she was different. As soon as she was old enough to speak, she insisted she was a girl. Luckily, Jazz has a very supportive family who helped her understand that she was born transgender. A transgender person is born one sex but identifies as the opposite gender.

Before Jazz knew she was transgender, she wore dresses in the house, but dressed like a boy outside. That all changed when, at the age of five, she wore a girl's bathing suit to a pool party and told everybody she was a girl. By the time Jazz was six, she was doing television interviews and raising awareness about what her life was like. This made her the youngest person to talk publicly about what it meant to be transgender. She wanted other transgender kids like her to know that their feelings were normal and that they were not alone.

As more people heard about Jazz, she began using social media to connect with her fans. On her YouTube channel, she talks to her thirty-three thousand followers about what it is like to be transgender and how others can be supportive. By the time she turned fourteen, she was named a Human Rights Campaign Youth Ambassador. That same year, a children's book titled *I Am Jazz* was published about her. Now Jazz has her own TV show, also called *I Am Jazz*, which offers a peek inside her life. Fans can't get enough of Jazz's bubbly personality and amazing spirit.

But not everybody understands Jazz. Many people have judged and bullied her and her family. Fortunately, she doesn't let these people get to her. She helped cofound TransKids Purple Rainbow Foundation to offer additional support to transgender children and has even written her own book, called *Being Jazz*.

Jazz's message is to always stay positive. She hopes that by speaking out, people will become more accepting of one another's differences.

SERENA: 1981–   VENUS: 1980–

VENUS *and* SERENA WILLIAMS

ATHLETES

Two of the most famous tennis pros in the world are not only good friends—they're also sisters! Venus and Serena Williams are a year apart and have loved tennis since they were little kids growing up in Compton, California. Venus, the older of the two, began playing tennis at the age of four, and Serena started at three. The courts they played on were filled with potholes, and nets were often missing, but that didn't stop the sisters from doing what they loved.

By the time the girls were seven and eight, they were devoting all their time to tennis. They moved to Florida to enroll in a tennis academy, where they trained six hours a day, six days a week, for four years. With their father managing their schedule, they began playing junior tournaments. Venus quickly became known for her powerful serve, which topped one hundred miles per hour! By the time the sisters were teenagers, they'd both landed twelve-million-dollar deals with athletic companies.

Some sisters might be driven apart by all the competition, but not these two. Venus and Serena celebrate each other's wins. And there are plenty! Venus has won Wimbledon—the most challenging tennis tournament in the world—five times. Serena has won Wimbledon seven times. Both sisters have won Olympic gold medals, and they sometimes team up to play doubles against other tennis pros. In 2016, the sisters won their sixth Wimbledon doubles title.

Some of the sisters' best games have been against each other. As of 2018, the two have played each other twenty-nine times. Serena has the lead, winning seventeen to twelve. No matter who wins, they are always proud of each other.

While tennis takes up most of their time, the sisters also enjoy other activities. They're into fashion, design, and acting, and they are the first African American women to be part owners of the Miami Dolphins football team. These two pros have so much passion that people who don't even like tennis love to watch them play.

1819–1896

CLARA SCHUMANN

MUSICIAN

Clara Wieck's father was a piano teacher and her mother was a concert pianist, so it was no surprise that Clara had a knack for music. From a young age, Clara was given lessons in piano, violin, and singing. In 1830, at just eleven years old, she performed a piano solo for the first time. This was unusual because, at the time, women did not perform in public, no matter how good they were. Not only that, but few women wrote their own music. Clara did both! She was so talented, her father became her manager and set up tours in Germany, where they lived, and all across Europe. Her shows sold out and critics loved her. By the time Clara was sixteen, she was famous. Some people even referred to her as the Queen of Piano.

Clara stood out from other famous musicians because she was a young girl. But she was also one of the first musicians ever to play music from memory. She played the music that she wrote herself and the music of other great composers.

Clara also played music written by a man named Robert Schumann, one of her father's students. He had injured his hand and couldn't play in public, so Clara performed his pieces for him. Clara and Robert spent a lot of time together and soon fell in love. Her father didn't approve of the relationship. He was sure that if they got married, it would mean the end of Clara's career because most married women didn't work in those days. But Clara was determined to marry Robert no matter what.

Disproving her father's fears, Clara continued to perform and write music after her marriage. Even though she had eight children and a husband to care for, she still found time to perform. After Robert died at a young age, Clara used the money she made from her concerts to support her family.

In her later years, Clara became a music teacher. She died at age seventy-six, leaving behind a musical legacy.

1996–

"The need was there, so now I'm working to fill it. That's my mission."

EASTON LACHAPPELLE

ROBOTICS ENGINEER

From an early age, Easton LaChappelle was taking apart pieces of equipment and putting them back together. He wanted to find out how everything worked and then use what he learned to come up with new inventions. When he was fourteen, he gathered LEGOs and fishing wire and made his first robotic hand.

Easton entered the robotic hand in the Colorado State Science Fair and won third place, but something more important happened that day. At the fair, he met a seven-year-old girl who was missing an arm. She had an artificial, or fake, limb that cost $80,000. This limb could open and close but couldn't move freely otherwise. Easton went home that day vowing to make a lighter, stronger, more moveable, and cheaper artificial limb.

Easton taught himself the technology and used the Internet to learn about electronics, computer coding, and 3-D printing. He made many models and soon came up with one that could be controlled with the brain, using advanced technology. Another model was so strong, it could hold up to fifty pounds with one finger. The best part was, he could sell these limbs for under $500.

NASA invited Easton to come work for them when he was seventeen. He was given a job working on the Robonaut, a robot that helps astronauts in space. Around the same time, Easton opened his own business called Unlimited Tomorrow, Inc. His mission was to use the latest technology to help amputees at a low cost to them. At age nineteen, Easton was invited to the White House, where he shook hands with President Obama using his robotic arm!

Today, Easton is still coming up with new ideas. He is currently working on a project that will allow paralyzed people to walk again. He knows that with the use of technology, he can make a big difference.

1939–

CLAUDETTE COLVIN

ADVOCATE FOR EQUALITY

One afternoon, Claudette Colvin was riding a city bus home from school when the driver told her to give up her seat to a white woman. As an African American living in Alabama during the 1950s, Claudette did not have the same rights as white people. She knew she was being treated unfairly because of her skin color and refused to give up her seat. This was the first time in history a black woman had dared to speak out against the unfair practice of segregation.

The bus driver called the police, who arrested Claudette and threw her in jail even though she was just fifteen years old. She was frightened, not knowing what would happen next. Her mother and pastor picked her up and brought her home, but Claudette wasn't about to give up her fight to end segregation. She went to court for her case and reminded the judge that all people are created equal.

The court voted against her, and since she was young and from a poor family, not many people heard her story. A year later, she was called to court to testify in another court case about segregation on buses. This case was called *Browder versus Gayle*, and it went all the way to the Supreme Court—the highest court in the United States. The final ruling on the case was that bus segregation in the state of Alabama must end! Claudette's courage to speak out finally paid off.

Now that Claudette was well known in her community, many employers were afraid to hire her. They didn't want to bring trouble to their businesses. Unable to get a job in Alabama, Claudette moved to New York to live with her older sister. She found a job in a nursing home, where she worked for thirty-five years before retiring in 2004.

Many people never had the chance to hear about Claudette Colvin. That's because nine months after she refused to give up her seat on the bus, another brave woman named Rosa Parks was arrested for the same crime and got more attention from the media because she was an adult. It's important to remember that Claudette's bravery helped others follow in her footsteps.

1998–

"I believe that the most powerful tool we have to overcome the inequalities and challenges children and young people—especially for those affected by conflict—face today is knowledge and education."

MUZOON ALMELLEHAN

ACTIVIST FOR GIRLS' RIGHTS AND EDUCATION

Muzoon Almellehan was fourteen years old when she and her family fled their home in Syria because of a civil war. They escaped to Jordan, where Muzoon, her three siblings, and her parents lived in refugee camps for three years.

Muzoon loved to learn and was able to attend school at the camps. But after a while, she began to notice that fewer and fewer girls were showing up to class. Muzoon soon learned that many parents were forcing their daughters to drop out of school and get married. Parents thought that this was the best way to ensure their daughters' safety and futures. Muzoon valued education and wanted to make sure other people also understood its importance. She began going around the camp, encouraging girls and their parents to make education a priority. Many rejected this idea, but Muzoon was persistent. She explained to the families that a good education meant more choices later on.

While at the camp, Muzoon met Malala Yousafzai, a well-known young activist who was also fighting for girls' rights. At the time, Malala was visiting the camp to help spread awareness about Syrian refugees. The two young women became friends, and it wasn't long before many people began calling Muzoon the Malala of Syria.

At the age of seventeen, Muzoon and her family moved to England, where she enrolled in high school. One good aspect of the move was that she was reunited with Malala, who also lives in England! The two of them have plans to work together to continue fighting for girls' and women's rights. Two years after moving, Muzoon made history when she became the youngest Goodwill Ambassador for UNICEF, a global organization that protects the rights of children. Muzoon wants to be a journalist when she grows up and hopes to one day return to Syria when the war is over to help rebuild the country.

❯❯ WHAT NOW? ❮❮

You've now read about some of the most amazing kids in the world. Some of them were born with special gifts and talents and worked hard to improve their natural skills. For others, their stories began with curiosities that then blossomed into passion projects. Through dedication and determination, all of these kids were able to see their dreams become realities—and their impact has made the world a better place for all of us.

And now it's your turn! What are you interested in? What are you good at? Where do you see a need in your community? You don't have to do it alone. Most of the kids in this book were successful because they had help from their family and friends. Rally the people around you to brainstorm ideas. And remember, as we've seen through the stories in this book, making a difference can take almost any form. Don't be afraid to pursue music, charity, science, art, literature, sports, or something totally outside the box!

Are YOU ready to make a difference?

Sources

The quotations used in this publication have been sourced from the following:

Almellehan, Muzoon. "International Youth Day is a Chance to Push for Children's Education." *TeenVogue*. Aug. 12, 2017. https://bit.ly/D19Sm9.

Bridges, Ruby. *Junior Scholastic*. By Abigayle Lista. Nov. 22, 2010. https://bit.ly/2GAl4un.

Clarke, Erika, and Kathleen Toner. "Teen's vision: Help children see clearer." *CNN*. Sept. 5, 2013. https://cnn.it/2utyZOq.

Comăneci, Nadia. *Laureus Sport for Good*. July 21, 2016. https://bit.ly/2DYcsbF.

"Dylan Mahalingam." *Huffington Post*. https://bit.ly/2GzAnU8.

"Emma Watson at the HeForShe Campaign 2014 – Official UN Video." *YouTube*, uploaded by United Nations. Sep. 22, 2014. https://bit.ly/1qpJRgG.

Frank, Anne. "Give! (March 26, 2944)." *Anne Frank Fonds*. https://bit.ly/2IZxpqc.

Goodman, Ellen. "Farewell To Samantha Smith, The Child Who Spoke For Us All." *Chicago Tribune*. Aug. 30, 1985. https://trib.in/2GfxkkM.

"HALO Award Honoree Nicholas Lowinger Talks Gotta Have Sole!" *Sweety High*. Nov. 17, 2014. https://bit.ly/2IZCBKI.

Hinton, S. E. *Book Reporter*. By Cindy Lynn Speer and Wiley Saichek. Oct. 8, 2004. https://bit.ly/2DWhQfn.

"Interview: Thandiwe Chama." *YouTube*, uploaded by UNECOSOC. Feb. 17, 2015. https://bit.ly/2I8sxOI.

"Interview with Elvis Presley – 28 August 1956." From *Elvis Answers Back!* magazine. Elvis100Percent.com. Accessed Mar. 27, 2018. https://bit.ly/2Ibgu30.

Jewell, Wendy. "Ryan Hreljac." *MY HERO*. Aug. 13, 2014. https://myhero.com/RYAN_HRELJAC.

Jones, Brian, and Harrison Jacobs. "That time 16-year-old Malala Yousafzai left Jon Stewart speechless with a comment about pacifism." *Business Insider*. June 18, 2015. https://read.bi/2IXVSML.